All about
JUSTIN BIEBER
100% UNOFFICIAL

PaRragon

Bath • New York • Singapore • Hong Kong • Cologne • Delhi
Melbourne • Amsterdam • Johannesburg • Auckland • Shenzhen

MY WORLD

BELIEBERS ONLINE:
8,000,000+ Twitter followers!

Facts

Full name:	Justin Drew Bieber
Nicknames:	J-Beebs, Biebz, JB
Height:	5'6"
Born:	March 1, 1994, at 12:56 a.m., on a Tuesday
Star sign:	Pisces
Pet:	Papillon dog named Sammy
Celeb crush:	Beyoncé
Hometown:	Stratford, Ontario, Canada

News & Secrets

Me Plus You

Justin's first single, "One Time," was written by the same people who wrote "Umbrella" for Rihanna and "Single Ladies" for Beyoncé.

Holla!

Bieber Cash

Wow! Most recent figures show that the Biebz may top **$112 million!** That'll buy a few pairs of high tops.

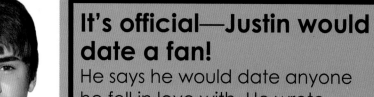

Fan News Just In

It's official—Justin would date a fan!

He says he would date anyone he fell in love with. He wrote "U Smile" for his amazing Beliebers and dedicates it to them all.

 I ♥ JB

Justin's Faves

Color:	Blue, but purple to wear
Movie:	All the Rocky movies
Sports team:	Toronto Maple Leafs
Hero:	Chuck Norris
Candy:	Sour Patch® Kids
Drink:	VitaminWater™
Food:	Spaghetti and meatballs

Bieberspeak Dictionary

Leggo = Let's go!

Swag = the way you carry yourself, with super-cool confidence!

Shawty = hot girl

Belieber = a crazy number 1 Justin fan

OMB! = Oh My Bieber!

NEVER SAY NEVER

Justin started out as just a normal kid from Stratford, Ontario—now he's one of the most famous people on the planet. Here are his five steps to swaggin' success ...

1. Dude Got Talent

Justin must have been drummin' to the beat from birth! He had serious rhythm, even when he was two years old.

At 12 he enjoyed singing around the house, but few people knew about his musical talent. He entered a local competition called Stratford Idol and sang in public for the first time, competing against trained singers—and managed to come in third! Some family and friends hadn't been able to make it, so his mom, Pattie, posted the video on YouTube ...

2. Social Media ... C'mon!

Justin got so many hits on YouTube that he started posting more videos of himself performing songs by artists like Usher, Ne-Yo, and Stevie Wonder.

Soon, people all over the world were logging on to watch this amazing lil' singer from Stratford. It wasn't long before he was getting thousands of hits, and later ... millions!

 3. Brains and ... Braun!

That's where Scooter Braun comes in. Justin had become huge without management or publicity, but to become a real star he was going to need a manager. A few months after Justin started posting videos, Scooter flew 13-year-old Justin to Atlanta to meet with people from the music biz.

4. OMB, It's Usher!

Scooter took Justin to a studio and they bumped into Usher—but Usher kinda blew Justin off, thinking he was just Scooter's little cousin! Months later, he saw Justin on YouTube and was like, "Man, I need to get this kid back!" Usher knew that Justin had the voice, talent, and charisma to make it. In October 2008, Justin was signed to Island Records.

5. Find Your Wolf Pack

Success is great, but having the right team around Justin was so important to help him stay at the top and keep him grounded. Justin's team is totally tight, and they're real careful about who they let in.

JUSTIN'S TEAM

Scooter Braun—manager and beast!
Usher—mentor and superstar
Ryan Good—stylist, road dog, and swagger coach
Kenny Hamilton—bodyguard and personal security ninja
Jamaica Craft—choreographer
Mama Jan—vocal coach (and "secret sauce," as Scooter says)
Jenny—homeschool tutor
Dan Kanter—lead guitarist and musical director

COULD YOU BE THE "ONE LESS LONELY GIRL"?

You'd probably settle for being in the same room as Justin, right? Find out how you would cope being right next to him on stage by answering YES or NO to the questions below.

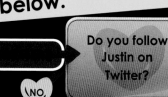

Do you follow Justin on Twitter?

NO → Have you seen the Biebz in concert?

YES → Have you practiced your Mrs. Bieber signature?

NO → Have you watched all of his old videos on YouTube?

YES → Is Justin's birthday written in your calendar?

NO → Is Justin's birthday written in your calendar?

YES → Do you know the name of every member of his team?

NO → Do you check the Net daily for the latest Bieber gossip?

YES → Is Justin's birthday written in your calendar?

YES → Have you watched *Never Say Never* more than ten times?

NO → Would you still love Justin if he wasn't famous?

YES → Would you still love Justin if he wasn't famous?

NO → **YES** →

Gigglin' girl

NO

You'd be a bag of gigglin' nerves if you got a spot on the "Lonely Girl" stool ... Luckily Justin likes a girl with a nice smile! And if you can make him laugh, too, you're on to a winner!

Screamin' sis

YES / **NO**

There is no way you can play this one cool. You're so super-excited that by the time you've left the stage, Justin won't be able to hear for a week! Maybe you'll hear him sing when you stop to take a breath!

Cryin' cutie

NO / **YES**

Awww, sweet! You're such a mega fan of the Biebz that getting up close might just be a bit much for you. But remember what Justin says—it's good to show your feelings, so don't hold back.

Sweet tweets

**Belieber followers alert!
Check out some of Justin's
top tweets of all time ...**

Update >

Justinbieber when Will Smith looks at you and says "I know movies and that's a hit movie" u just feel good. What a night. No words other than #thankyou

JADEN SMITH SAYS HIS DAD DOESN'T PUT HIM IN WACK MOVIES, BUT NEVER SAY NEVER 3D ROCKS!

Justinbieber Yeah so it's true...i got a lil haircut...i like it... and we are giving all the hair cut to CHARITY to auction. Details coming soon.

JUSTIN LOST 80,000 TWITTER FOLLOWERS WHEN HE CHOPPED HIS FAMOUS BIEBER 'DO—BUT HE RAISED $40,668 FOR CHARITY!

Justinbieber rehearsed for the #grammys with @ usherraymond and jaden. feeling good. cant believe we are at the #grammys—this is nuts!

JUSTIN GAVE A ROCKIN' PERFORMANCE AT THE GRAMMYS!
TOO BAD HE MISSED OUT ON AN AWARD THOUGH!

Justinbieber If i could RT, FOllow, and reply 2 all of u i would. Im beyond grateful 2 u 4 ur never ending support & sticking by me and my music. thanks

JUSTIN'S FANS ARE THE MOST LOYAL EVER!

Justinbieber Im never gonna change...i will always remember...i will always be that kid from stratford...I will always be grateful.

AND THAT'S WHAT WE LOVE MOST ABOUT THE BIEBZ. <3

FAMILY COMES FIRST

Life's a trip for Justin, but he needs people who've got his back ... He knows family always comes first.

Justin didn't have the easiest time growing up, especially when his mom and dad separated. He says, "No kid likes to have their parents split up. You don't get to see them together, but I got two Christmases, which is always a bonus ..." Being raised by a single mother and living in low-income housing was tough, but it just made Justin stronger.

Mom: Pattie Mallette

"I love my mom—she's awesome."

Dad: Jeremy Bieber

"I have a great relationship with my dad."

Justin wrote his song "Down to Earth" about his parents' divorce.

Before he became famous, Justin used to perform on the front steps of a theater in Stratford. His mom worked so hard to support him that he decided to save for an extra-special gift ... "I often sat with my guitar and sang. After a while I got so many tips ($3,000!) that I could pay for the first-ever vacation for my mom and me. We went to Florida!"

Justin spent a lot of his childhood at his grandparents' house. He had his own room there, painted blue and white with Toronto Maple Leafs stuff all over the walls. Justin may be taller than his grandpa now, but he says he'll always look up to him!

Grandparents: Bruce and Diane Dale
"We were poor but my grandparents spoiled me."

Justin has two half siblings from his dad's second marriage: Lil' sis Jazmyn calls Justin "Bieber" and is the one person who can always make him smile!

Lil' bro and sis: Jazmyn and Jaxon
"I would do anything for them."

Justin's mom travels with him wherever he goes, 24/7. They're really close, but even stars argue with their parents! Justin says, "When you go to school, you get away from your mom for a while, but I'm not at school so we bump heads a bit!"

Justin's dad has been a big influence on his life and music, and taught him some of his first tunes on the guitar. Now that Justin is mega rich, he's bought a new home for his dad and wants to help Jeremy launch his own career as a rapper. Look out for "Lord Bieber"!

DOWN TO EARTH

Justin's still that same boy from Stratford ... and this is how we know!

His mom still grounds him if he acts up!

If Justin steps out of line, he might have his phone or computer taken away. One time he wouldn't give up his phone, so Pattie just canceled his calling plan instead!

He still has to clean his own room!

Did you see in Never Say Never when Justin's grandma tells him he can't go out until he cleans his room? In front of his friends, too!

He still has the same best buddies!

Ryan Butler and Chaz Somers have been Justin's best friends since they played hockey together when they were little. Ryan appears in Justin's "One Time" music video—which they filmed in Usher's house! It's Ryan playing video games with Justin at the start.

His mom looks after his money!

Justin doesn't even really get an allowance. When he wants to get something, he has to ask his mom!

His pals look out for him!

Usher hired his old friend Ryan to watch over Justin, and of course Scooter keeps Justin's pranks under control!

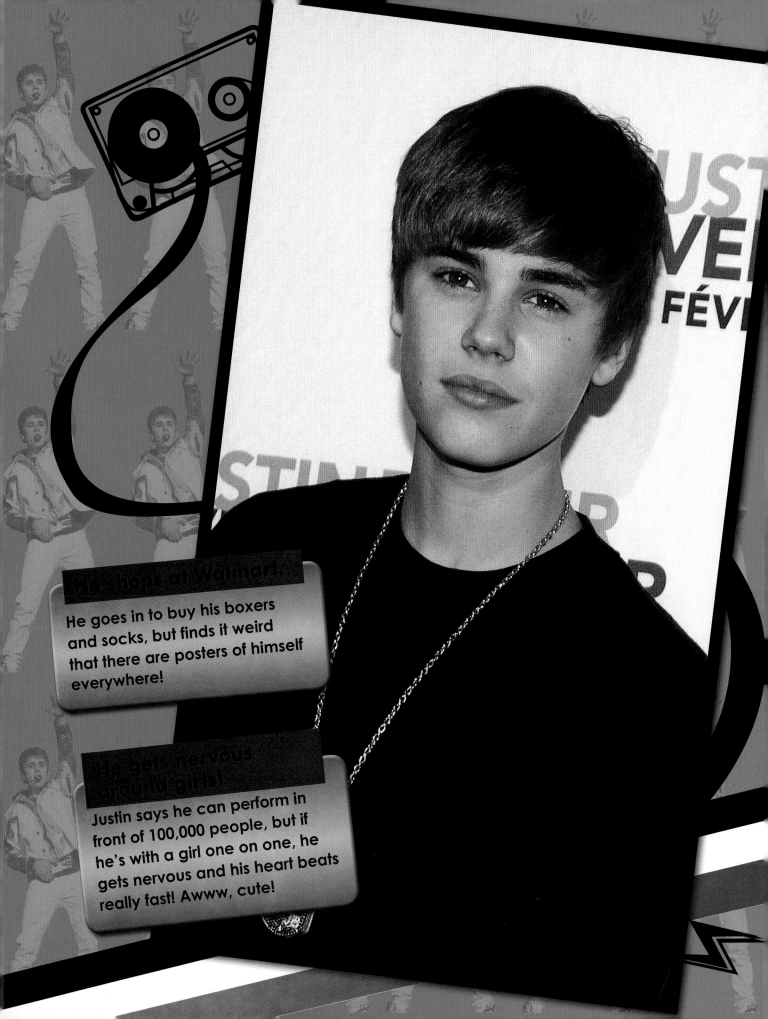

He shops at Walmart.

He goes in to buy his boxers and socks, but finds it weird that there are posters of himself everywhere!

He gets nervous around girls!

Justin says he can perform in front of 100,000 people, but if he's with a girl one on one, he gets nervous and his heart beats really fast! Awww, cute!

RU A TRUE BELIEBER?

Take the JB pop quiz! Pick your answer then check your score to find out how much you really Beliebe!

1. Which of these artists is Justin's ultimate music idol?

A. Michael Jackson

B. Lady Gaga

C. Mariah Carey

2. What was the first song that Justin recorded in an actual recording studio?

A. "One Less Lonely Girl"

B. "Eenie Meenie"

C. "Common Denominator"

3. What song did Miley Cyrus sing with Justin in *Never Say Never*?

A. "Up"

B. "Overboard"

C. "Somebody to Love"

4. Which act was Justin supporting when he tripped on stage and broke his foot?

A. The Jonas Brothers

B. Miley Cyrus

C. Taylor Swift

5. What number did "Baby" reach in the charts?

A. 8

B. 3

C. 5

6. What does Justin say were the longest three minutes of his life?

A. Performing for President Obama

B. Waiting for L. A. Reid, the record executive, to say he was signed

C. When he broke his foot on stage and had to finish his song

7. What was the one thing Justin really wanted to know when he was signing his record deal?

A. Do I get a tour bus?

B. Do I get to meet Beyoncé?

C. Can I tell everyone at school?

8. What song was at number 1 on the Billboard Hot 100 when Justin was born?

A. "Always," Bon Jovi

B. "The Power of Love," Celine Dion

C. "All I Wanna Do," Sheryl Crow

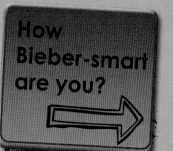

How Bieber-smart are you? ➡

0–2 correct: Bieber Beginner!

You know the basics, but being a top fan is tough and you've got a little more reading and YouTube surfin' to do before you're a Bieber expert.

Homework: Sing along to your fave Bieber tune until you know all the words.

3–5 correct: Bieberitis

Wow, you know Justin really well, but you've got a little more Beliebing to do before you can be a number 1 fan.

Homework: Practice your Mrs. Bieber signature. You never know when you might need it!

6–8 correct: Bieber Fever!

We better take your temperature because your Bieber Fever is off the chart! You're living in Bieberland and probably don't have time for much else.

Homework: Maybe some real schoolwork, eh?

I ♥ JB

Love love love!

Answers: 1.A, 2.C, 3.B, 4.C, 5.C, 6.C, 7.A, 8.B.

TRICKS AND TALENTS

You've heard of "triple threats"—people who can sing, dance, and act? Well, what do you call someone who can do all of that AND MORE? Bieberrific, of course!

Music ...

Justin says, "I started playing drums when I was two, guitar when I was seven, and piano when I was five. I taught myself to play all of them."

When Justin got a little bigger, some of his mom's friends pulled a benefit together to help him buy a real set of drums. Awesome! He had to blast the stereo at top volume when he played along with his fave tunes.

Singing ...

Until Justin signed his record deal, he had never had a vocal coach. He just learned by listening to famous singers, like Boyz II Men, and trying to copy their style. Oh yeah, and he can rap, too!

Acting ...

Justin made his acting debut on *CSI*. Fans of the show were blown away by his performance. He was literally blown away when he was shot dead in his second episode!

Dancing ...

Justin's got some mad dance skills. Maybe it's because he's so good at sports. He can even do some breakdancing!

Surprise Skillz

Justin can solve a Rubik's cube in under a minute! He says there's a trick to it.

He can do his hair in under five minutes! MAJOR skill, lol!!

He can speak fluent French and even went to a French-speaking school for a while.

WHICH BIEB SONG MAKES U SMILE? ☺

Which of these three Bieber songs is your perfect match?

START HERE →

"Down To Earth" or "Pray"? — **Down** → Long Bieber 'do or short Bieber 'do? — **Short** → Justin on drums or on piano?

"Down To Earth" or "Pray"? ↓ **Pray**

Long Bieber 'do or short Bieber 'do? ↓ **Long**

Justin on drums or on piano? ↓ **Drums**

Justin on drums or on piano? — **Piano** → Ryan Good or Scooter Braun?

Rihanna or Beyoncé? — **Rihanna** → Ryan Good or Scooter Braun? — **Ryan** → Pandas or zebras?

Rihanna or Beyoncé? ↓ **Beyoncé**

Ryan Good or Scooter Braun? ↓ **Scooter**

Pandas or zebras? ↓ **Zebras**

Pandas or zebras? — **Pandas** → Purple or blue?

Willow or Jaden Smith? — **Jaden** → Purple or blue? — **Purple** → Sing with Justin or dance with Justin?

Willow or Jaden Smith? ↓ **Willow**

Purple or blue? ↓ **Blue**

Sing with Justin or dance with Justin? ↓ **Dance**

Sing with Justin or dance with Justin? — **Sing** →

♪ "Baby"

You've been a fan of Justin since the start, and would love to be his baby! You're a super-sweet person and you've always got your friends' backs.

♪ "Never Say Never"

This tune's got everything—awesome melody, cool rap by Jaden, and a really good message. You're really determined and won't give up on your dreams.

♪ "Somebody To Love"

You like a good dancin' tune, and this one will always get the party started! You're really fun to be around, which is why you have such a big group of friends.

10 CRAZY THINGS YOU GOTTA KNOW ABOUT JUSTIN

1. Push your UGGs to the back of your closet! Justin thinks they're too big and clumpy! "UGGs are ugg-ly!" he says.

2. Justin is scared of elevators since he got stuck in one for hours when he was younger.

3. J-Beebs has both ears pierced—but doesn't really ever wear earrings!

4. Remember when Justin broke his foot on stage with Taylor Swift? He broke the same foot the year before when he was skateboarding!

5. If Justin hadn't been a superstar pop prince, he would have put his love of drawing to good use as ... an architect!

6. He says one of the craziest things he's ever been given by a fan is some Cap'n Crunch cereal!

7. The video for "Baby," featuring Ludacris, broke records as being the world's most viewed YouTube video—ever!

8. Justin doesn't own a wallet! And he doesn't really carry cash around—he just stuffs his credit card into his pocket.

9. His tour was so big that it took 11 buses for all the people, 9 trucks for the equipment, 30 towels used on stage for each show, and 1 million pieces of confetti every night!

10. Justin has bodyguards with him 24/7. The only time he's on his own is when he goes to the bathroom! :O

HOLLA, SPORTS FANS!

So we all know Justin as this amazing musician, but when he was back home, people actually knew him better for his sports skills!

Baseball

Justin loves baseball, so he made a smart decision about the music video for the acoustic version of "Never Say Never" ... They filmed it in Angel Stadium and it debuted before a World Series game!

Skateboarding

Justin says he's "pretty good, but not awesome" at skateboarding. When he was on tour in England he even jumped on his skateboard in the airport! Swag!

Soccer

Justin played soccer for his local team, the Stratford Strikers. He had some pretty impressive moves. One time he got talking to soccer star David Beckham when he was watching a b-ball game.

Justin even tried bungee jumping in New Zealand!

Hockey

Justin is **crrr-a-a-a-a-a-zy** about hockey! It's his favorite sport of all time, and he is a huge fan of the Toronto Maple Leafs. It's also how he met his two best friends, Chaz Somers and Ryan Butler, because when they were seven or eight they played local league hockey together. After hockey they would go down to his grandparents' basement and try out professional wrestling moves! Remember the stuffed fox with the broken leg in *Never Say Never*?!

Justin's sports idol is hockey legend Wayne Gretzky. Wayne gave him a Team Canada hockey jersey!

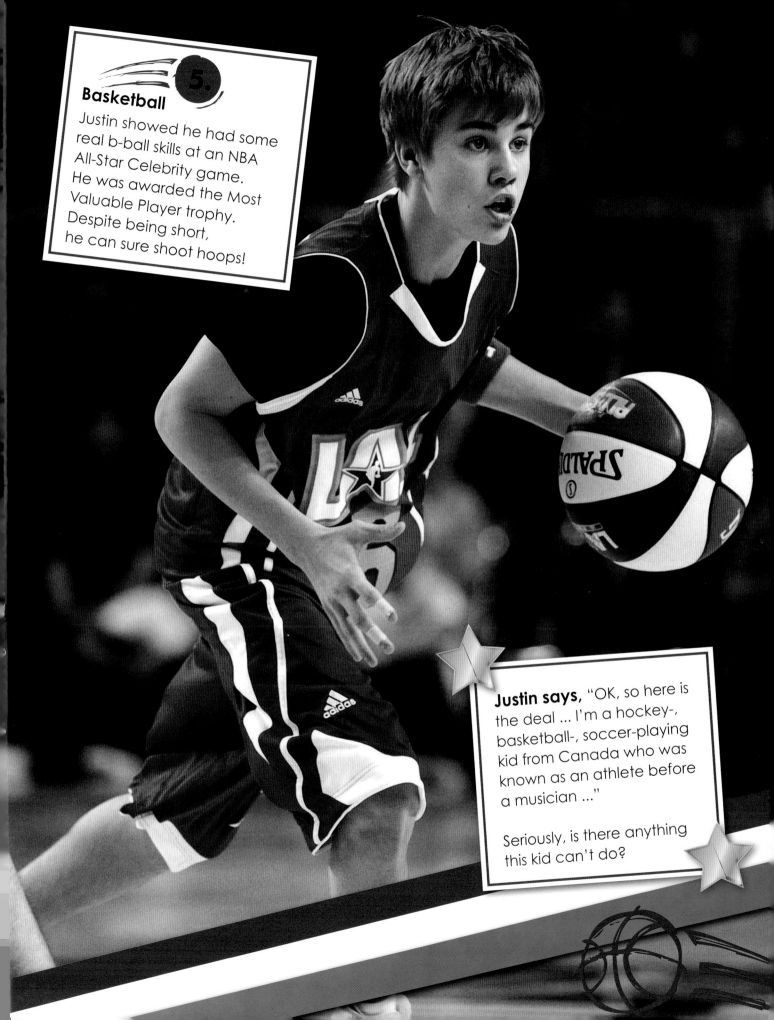

Basketball

5.

Justin showed he had some real b-ball skills at an NBA All-Star Celebrity game. He was awarded the Most Valuable Player trophy. Despite being short, he can sure shoot hoops!

Justin says, "OK, so here is the deal ... I'm a hockey-, basketball-, soccer-playing kid from Canada who was known as an athlete before a musician ..."

Seriously, is there anything this kid can't do?

BIEBER GOT SWAG

Let's give a big fist bump "wassup" to JB!
Justin really knows he's made it **big** 'cause ...

He's had his own wax figure made!

He got a **Range Rover** for his 16th birthday ... **from Usher!**

He has loadsa **celebrity girls** chasing after him!

He has **8 million** followers on **Twitter.**

He sang for the **President.**

When he told a reporter that his favorite candy was Sour Patch® Kids, he got thousands of bags sent to him and more thrown at him on stage!

At the premiere of his *Never Say Never* movie, the red carpets were changed to purple because it's his signature color!

He pretty much doesn't get nervous anymore, even though he's singing to crowds of thousands!

CELEB PHOTO WALL

 Like

Taylor Swift

Taylor Swift is one of Justin's "Favorite Girls" and was sweet to him when he broke his foot.

Miley Cyrus

Miley Cyrus has been through a lot of the same things as Justin, so they've become good friends.

Sean Kingston

Justin and Sean Kingston smash it on stage with "Eenie Meenie"!

Selena Gomez

Selena's smile and good sense of humor are why Justin wanted to date her. She's his first official celebrity girlfriend!

Rihanna

Rihanna's a total Belieber! She and JB have a lot of the same writers, so they're really close.

Jaden Smith

Jaden Smith and Justin have become best buddies ... Bromance!

Usher

Usher has done so much for Justin and was there from the start. As he said, "This is the first step to forever, man."

Willow Smith

Willow killed it as the opening act for Justin's tour. Jaden and Justin watched on like proud big bros!

FACT OR FAKED?

Justin has had to deal with his fair share of tough rumors. Now it's your turn to find out the truth about the gossip …

Justin once said he could take the Jonas Brothers on in a fight!

Fact!

Yep—all three! But he was just kidding around!

Justin is going to star in an episode of *Glee* dedicated to his songs.

Faked!

TV bosses say they won't do it until he has as many hit songs as Madonna or Britney.

Justin has a secret passion to learn to play the spoons.

Faked!

Lol, Justin's not into playing the spoons, but he did invent spoon swaggin' where he poses doing funny stuff with spoons! Random!

He had an embarrassing moment on his first-ever date.

Fact!

Justin took a girl to an Italian restaurant and dropped spaghetti down his shirt! But Justin can laugh about it now.

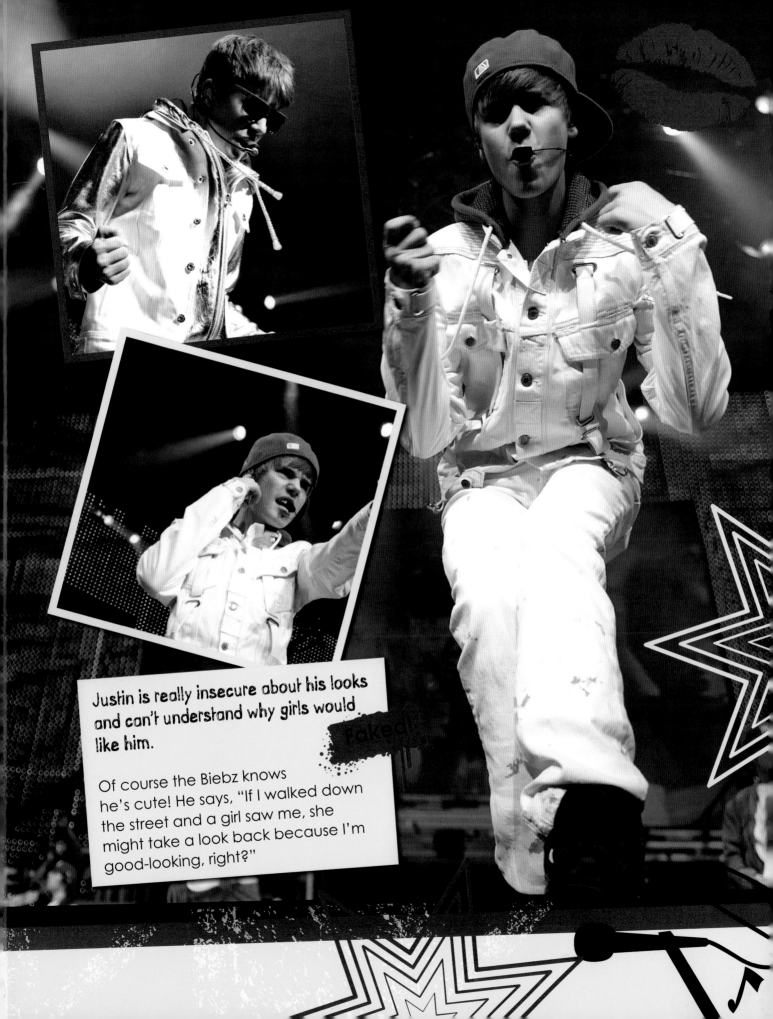

Justin is really insecure about his looks and can't understand why girls would like him.

Faked!

Of course the Biebz knows he's cute! He says, "If I walked down the street and a girl saw me, she might take a look back because I'm good-looking, right?"

WHY JUSTIN ♥'S HIS FANS

Justin Bieber's fans are the most important people in the world to him. Why? Because they found him and they help him to live his dream!

I ♥ JB

Giving Back

JB's loyal fans make it possible for him to help some amazing charities in some wild 'n' wacky ways …

Baby, It's Shoe!

The Biebz gave a signed purple Nike sneaker to Stratford Northwestern Secondary School in Ontario, his former school. They raised money to build a broadcasting and communications studio for students.

Birthday Gift

Awww, Justin has such a kind heart. Instead of presents for his 17th birthday, he asked friends, family, and fans if they would donate $17 to charity instead. They made over $40,000 for Charity Water, which brings clean, safe water to people in developing countries.

Hairy Situation!

The world gasped when Justin cut his famous Bieber 'do! But it was worth it … The eBay auction for a lock of his hair closed with a winning bid of $40,668! All proceeds went to support the Gentle Barn Foundation, a charity that rescues and rehabilitates animals.

What Justin says about his Beliebers …

"My fans really inspire me. I feed off their energy. If they're screaming loudly, I get pumped up and it's really exciting."

"Every day I wake up knowing I have the best fans in the world. Every day you go above and beyond for me, and I wanted to let you know that I know and I'm extremely appreciative every day."

 Belieber Warning!

When Justin was in Germany, four girls sneaked into a dumpster so they could get into his building! They were found by the garbage men. Ew … that trash would smell really bad!

Belieber Warning!

Some crazy fans got tattoos of "Never Say Never" to show their love for JB! Now that's pretty serious…

BIEBER KARAOKE!

Can you guess which fave JB song these lyrics come from … and then sing the next line?

1.

Are we an item?
Girl, quit playin'
"We're just friends,"
what are you sayin'?

2.

You seem like the type
to love 'em and
leave 'em
And disappear
right after this song

3.

I never thought I could
feel this power,
I never thought that I
could feel this free

4.

How many I told yous
and start overs and
shoulders have you
cried on before?

5.

Baby take my open
heart and all it offers
'Cause this is as
unconditional as
it'll ever get

6.

You're who I'm thinking
of, girl, you ain't my
runner-up

7.

No one has
a solid answer
But just walking
in the dark